3+

PIXAR

Take-Along
ABCs

D1510005

Ðɪꜱɴᴇʏ **LEARNING**

Carson Dellosa Education
Greensboro, North Carolina

Dᶦˢⁿᵉʸ **LEARNING**

COPYRIGHT © 2020 Disney Enterprises, Inc. and Pixar.
All rights reserved.

Disney/Pixar elements © Disney/Pixar; rights in underlying vehicles are
the property of the following third parties: Hudson Hornet, Hudson, and
Nash Ambassador are trademarks of FCA US LLC; FIAT is a trademark
of FCA Group Marketing S.p.A.; Ford Coupe is a trademark of Ford
Motor Company.

Published by
Carson Dellosa Education
PO Box 35665
Greensboro, NC 27425 USA

Trace and write.

aliens

Connect the As and as to finish the picture.
Then, color.

start

finish

4

Trace and write.

Buzz

B B B B

b b b b

Circle 3 pictures that start with B or b.

backpack

Bonnie

Bo

markers

Trace and write.

cone

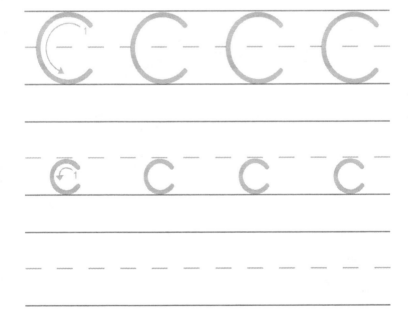

Connect the path of Cs and cs to help Cruz win the trophy!

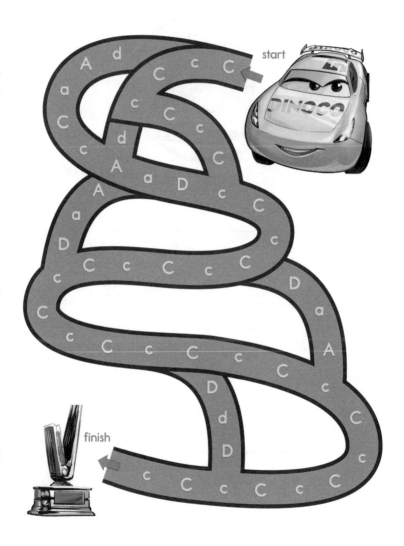

8

Trace and write.

Dory

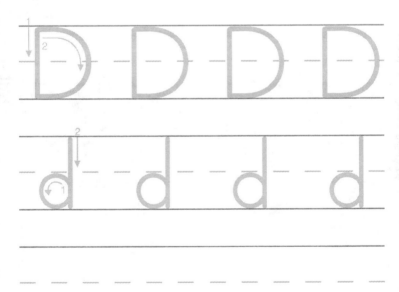

Find the 5 hidden Ds and ds.

10

Trace and write.

ears

Match the big letters to the small letters.

 **E**

 **e**

 **e**

 **E**

Trace and write.

Forky

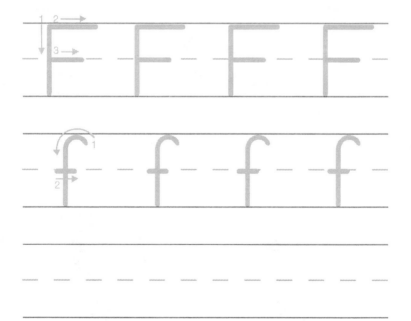

Draw a line to connect Forky to each trash can with F or f.

14

Trace and write.

gas

G G G G

g g g g

Write the missing letter in each pair.

Go!

G _____

_____ g

G _____

_____ g

Trace and write.

Hank

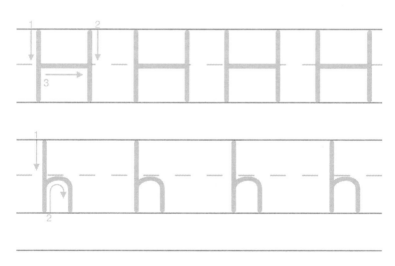

Connect the path of Hs and hs to finish the picture. Then, color.

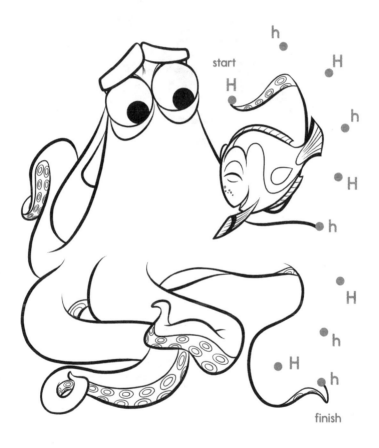

start

h

H

H

h

H

h

H

h

H

h

finish

Trace and write.

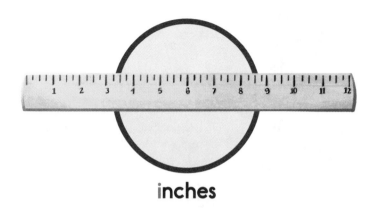

inches

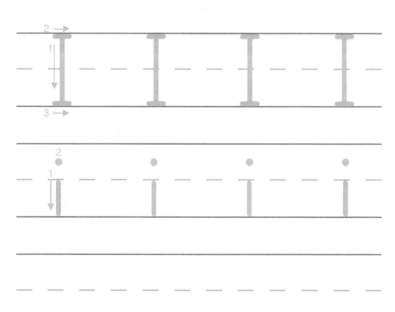

19

Circle each child with I or i.

i

I

i

L

F

Trace and write.

Jackson Storm

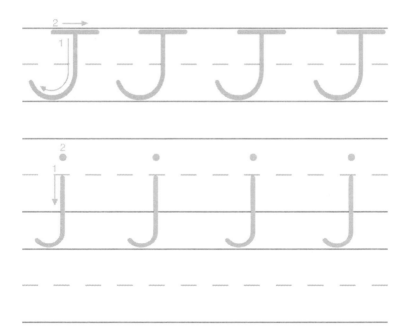

Color the **J**s and **j**s in each car's path. The car with the most **J**s and **j**s wins the race!

 j

 J

 H

 j

 J

 g

 J

 j

 g

 H

 j

g

Trace and write.

kids

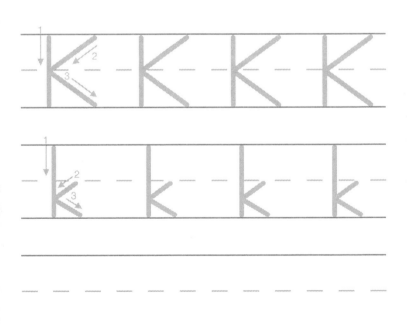

Match the big letters to the small letters.

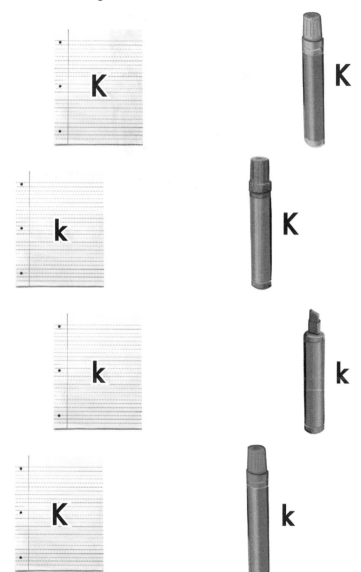

Trace and write.

Lightning McQueen

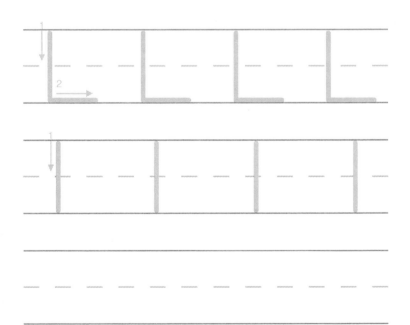

Connect the Ls and ls to finish the picture.
Then, color.

start

finish

Trace and write.

Marlin

Connect the path of Ms and ms to help Marlin and Nemo find Dory!

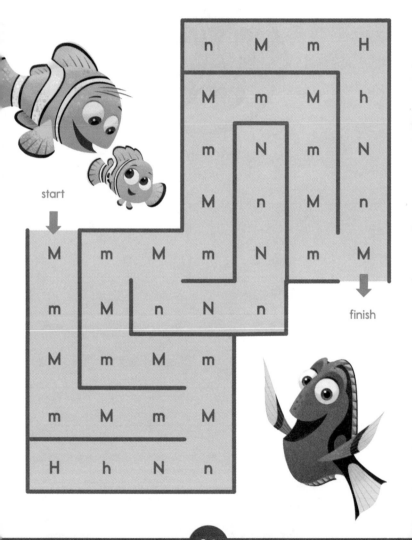

28

Trace and write.

Nemo

Connect the path of Ns and ns to finish the picture. Then, color.

N start

finish

Trace and write.

otter

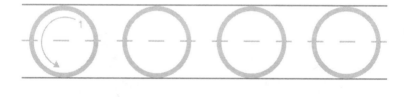

Circle the otters with O or o.

Trace and write.

Pearl

P P P P

p p p p

Circle all the fish swimming toward P or p.

34

Trace and write.

quick

Connect the path of Qs and qs to help Lightning McQueen get to his pit crew.

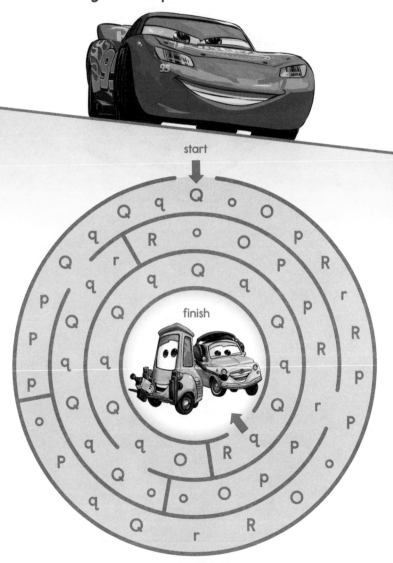

start

finish

Trace and write.

Rex

R R R R

r r r r r

Circle 3 pictures that start with R or r.

chalk

ball

rainbow

Rex

ruler

Trace and write.

sea lion

S - S - S - S

S - S - S - S

Connect the path of **S**s and **s**s to help Gerald find Rudder and Fluke.

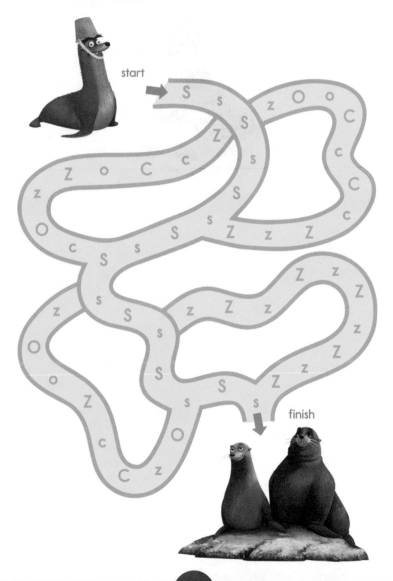

start

finish

Trace and write.

toys

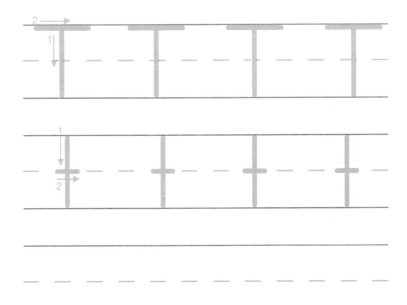

Trace the Ts and ts in the words below.

Bu____ercup

____rixie

Mr. Pricklepan____s

Trace and write.

underwater

Find 5 hidden Us and us.

Trace and write.

vase

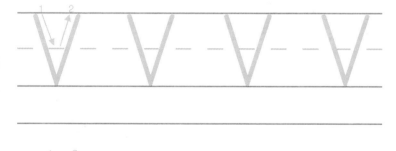

Circle the antiques with V or v.

Trace and write.

Woody

Connect the path of Ws and ws to help Woody find Forky.

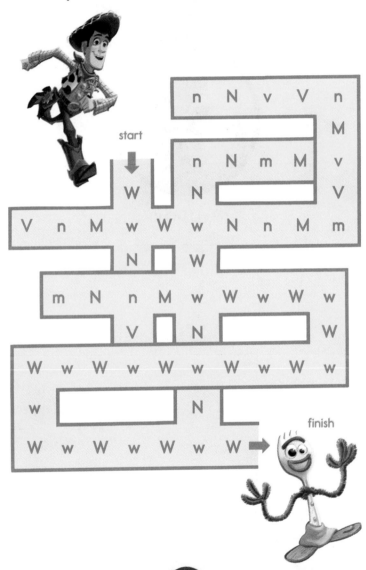

Trace and write.

box

Circle the barrels with **X** or **x**.

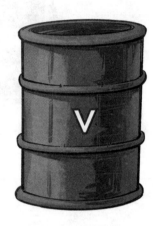

Trace and write.

y**arn**

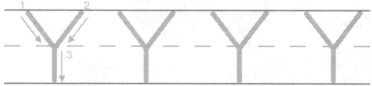

Find 5 hidden Ys and ys.

Trace and write.

zoom

Z Z Z Z

Z Z Z Z

Match the big letters to the small letters.

Find and circle 10 hidden letters.

Match the big letters to the small letters.

Connect the dots from a to z to finish the picture. Then, color.

start

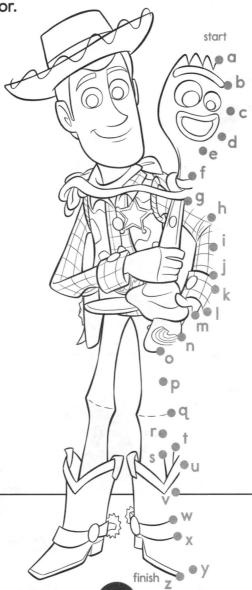

a
b
c
d
e
f
g
h
i
j
k
l
m
n
o
p
q
r
t
s
u
v
w
x
y
finish z

Connect the path from A to Z to help Dory find her parents!

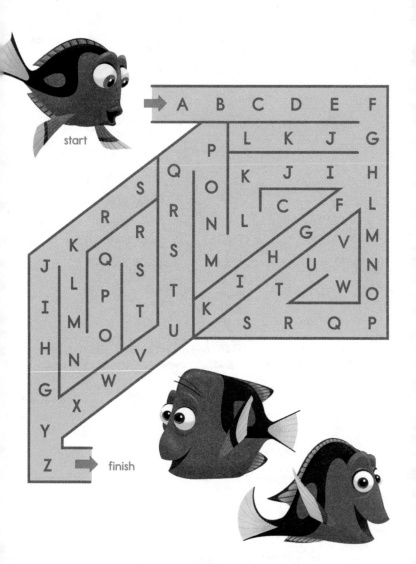

58

Now, write your name!

Page 4

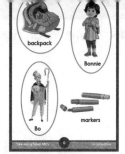

Page 6

Page 8

Page 10

Page 12

Page 14

Page 16

Page 18

Page 20

Page 22

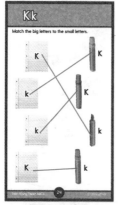

Page 24

Page 26

Page 28

Page 30

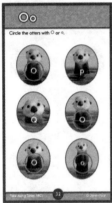

Page 32

Page 34

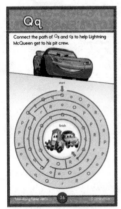

Page 36

Page 38

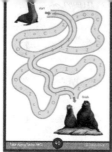

Page 40

Bu ‖ercup

‖rixie

Mr. Pricklepan ‖ s

Page 42

Uu

Find 5 hidden Us and us.

Page 44

Vv

Circle the antiques with V or v.

Page 46

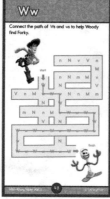

Ww

Connect the path of Ws and ws to help Woody find Forky.

Page 48

Xx

Circle the barrels with X or x.

Page 50

Page 52

Page 54

Page 55

Page 56

Page 57

Page 58